I0816208

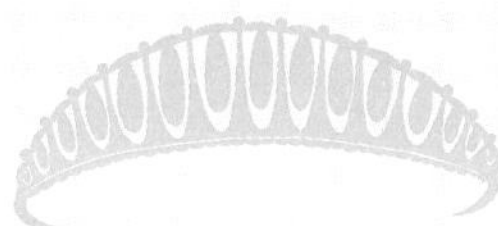

ORDINARY PEOPLE CHANGE THE WORLD

I am Princess Diana

BRAD MELTZER

illustrated by Christopher Eliopoulos

ROCKY POND BOOKS

I am **Princess Diana.**

I was born the third daughter to the Viscount and Viscountess Althorp.

Those are fancy titles that mean I was born into a wealthy British family.

It may sound like a fairy tale—
but you'll see, my life was no fairy tale.

Growing up, I adored animals.

I rode horses and had pet rabbits, hamsters, guinea pigs, a foul-tempered cat named Marmalade, and a dog named Jill!

I loved them so much, my bed was covered with twenty stuffed animals, leaving just a tiny space for me.

At Park House, we had our own swimming pool and tennis court, plus massive fields, parks, and lawns.

It really does look like a fairy tale, doesn't it?

But my childhood wasn't great.

My parents were loving and full of humor.

But they didn't hug me, and they never told me they loved me.

We rarely ate dinner together as a family.

My brother and I ate with my nanny in the nursery.

For Christmas, I'd be given a catalog from the fancy toy store.

I'd pick out whatever I wanted.

That may sound fun, but trust me, having lots of things will never replace being loved.

I wasn't the only one who was unhappy.

My parents were always arguing with each other.

It was sad and sometimes scary to hear it.

When I was five, I'd hide behind the door of the drawing room.

One of the most painful things in my life happened when I was six years old.

My parents got divorced.

That means they didn't want to be married or live together anymore.

During a divorce, it's important to know that your parents still love you.

But back then, no one explained that to me.

I'd sit outside, waiting for my mom to return.

I felt different—
and very alone.

Thankfully, I had my grandmother Countess Spencer. She was always sweet and kind—and not just to me.

She used to visit people in her town who were sick or needed something that they couldn't afford.

People say I look just like her. But she gave me more than my looks.

My grandmother taught me to be compassionate, which means when you see someone suffering, you want to help.

In school, I liked dancing, diving, tennis, and playing the piano, but I wasn't a great student.

In fact, back then, I remember thinking

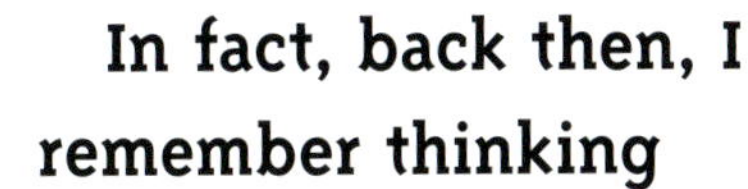

Thankfully, there was one thing I was really good at.

Every Tuesday and Thursday, a group of us would go to a local hospital for the mentally and physically disabled.

It had giant wooden doors, like a medieval castle.

When the doors opened, all these sick people would come toward us.

Some of my classmates would get scared,
but I was never scared when it came to helping people.

At the hospital, we learned to meet people where they were.

I didn't know it at the time, but there's a real power in holding someone's hand.

During one visit, the hospital put on music.
Since many of the patients were in wheelchairs, they couldn't stand and dance.
The other volunteers pushed them from behind.

I had a better idea.
I approached them face-to-face.
WOULD YOU LIKE TO JOIN ME?

We danced. Together.

What I was really doing was showing them empathy, which is when you imagine yourself in someone else's shoes so you understand what they're going through.

I was shy, happy spending nights at home, watching TV, and eating cereal.

That is, until one day, when I got a special invitation.

DIANA, YOU GOT INVITED TO A ROYAL HOUSE PARTY AT SANDRINGHAM!

MAYBE YOU'LL BE THE NEXT QUEEN OF ENGLAND!

SHE REALLY WAS SCRUBBING THE FLOOR WHEN IT CAME.

That weekend, at a separate barbeque, I was seated next to the queen's son—Prince Charles himself.

Since he was a prince, I was expected to call him sir.

Prince Charles and I began spending time together.

We even went on his royal yacht.

It did feel like a fairy tale.

When you're dating the future King of England—and fall in love—people take notice.

It became national news, and the press became interested in every part of my life.

From there . . .

Our wedding was watched on TV by 750 million people in more than 70 countries.

We got 47,000 letters of congratulations.

And 10,000 gifts.

I became Princess Diana, Her Royal Highness.

It seemed like the perfect life—but I had no idea what I was getting into. No idea.

As a princess, there are certain ways you're expected to act.

At charity events, most royal women wave politely . . .

Or extend a gloved hand.

You're not supposed to get down on your knees or get close.

I knew what it was like to feel different—and how important it was to be hugged.

A princess wasn't supposed to show her emotions.
I wasn't so good at that.

Over time, my popularity grew.
Crowds followed me wherever I went.

During my time in Kensington Palace, my greatest joys were my sons, William and Harry.

But there were hard times too.

Prince Charles and I found ourselves spending more and more time apart.

My priorities became my children and my charity work.

During one hospital visit, I saw a man watching over his wife. She was really sick, so I asked him . . .

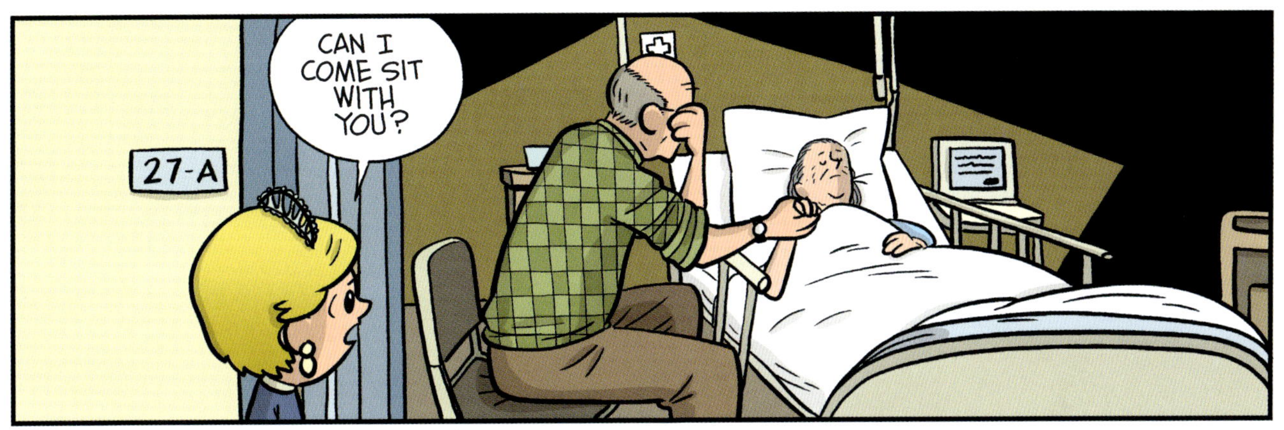

For two hours, I held his hand and his wife's hand. Sometimes people just want to know they're not alone.

Visits like that made me realize: Anywhere I saw suffering, that's where I wanted to be, doing what I can.

In November 1989, in Indonesia, I stood in 94° heat, shaking hands with people who had leprosy, a disease that makes your hands bent and bloodied, your body blistered.

No one wanted to touch these people.

I didn't hesitate.

And who had AIDS, a new and terrible disease that people didn't understand.

Back then, if you had AIDS, people were afraid they would catch it by being near you.

But we should never close our hearts like that.

During one visit to see AIDS patients, a man started crying when I held his hand.

I wanted to hug him, to make him feel better.

I reached out and squeezed him tight.

He squeezed me back, laughing with joy.

It's amazing what a hug can do.

Along the way, I learned how to take better care of myself, and how to get help when I felt sad or lonely.

I told the world it's okay to do the same.

As my sons got older, I also made sure to teach them the value of service.

We didn't always bring cameras.

Some of the best good deeds are never seen by anyone.

But they're never forgotten.

Eventually, Prince Charles and I separated and then got divorced.
The press was ruthless, making me feel like I was always being judged.

Daily
THURSDAY, FEBRUARY 29, 1996
NEWSPAPER OF THE YEAR 35p
DIVORCE

Leaving the royal family meant I wasn't an official princess anymore.
But you don't need to be a princess to help people.

DIANA, THERE ARE LEPROSY VICTIMS IN NEPAL...
NO ONE GOES TO SEE THEM.
THEY'RE ALL ALONE.
WE SHOULD GO.

Never forget, you always have the power to help others.

One of my most important missions was in Angola, Africa.

I found out seven children had been killed by land mines, which are explosive devices that soldiers bury in the ground during war.

The kids were playing soccer in a field that should've been cleared of the mines.

After my visit, 122 governments signed the Ottawa Treaty to stop using mines that could hurt innocent people.

My life was most definitely not a fairy tale.
I was taught not to show that I was sad,
or lonely,
or in pain.
Or even that I was joyful and full of love.
But when you keep your emotions inside,
it prevents you from connecting with others.

It can be hard—or even scary—to see someone suffering.
Sometimes, you may even want to turn away.
Do not turn away.
Offer a smile,
a hand,
or even a hug.
When you do . . .

It'll be your crowning achievement.
DIANA CAME TO BE KNOWN AS THE PEOPLE'S PRINCESS AND ONCE TOLD A GROUP OF 800 DOCTORS THAT "A HUG IS CHEAP, ENVIRONMENTALLY FRIENDLY, AND NEEDS MINIMAL INSTRUCTION."
IT'S STILL GREAT ADVICE.
NELSON MANDELA SAID SHE "TRANSFORMED PUBLIC ATTITUDES AND IMPROVED THE LIFE CHANCES" OF PEOPLE WITH AIDS AND OTHER DISEASES.
AFTER DIANA DIED IN A CAR CRASH BEING CHASED BY THE PRESS, THE OUTPOURING OF LOVE WAS SO STRONG, 6,000 LETTERS ARRIVED DAILY FILLED WITH DONATIONS TO HER MEMORIAL FUND.
THE FUND GAVE AWAY NEARLY $180 MILLION TO CHARITIES THAT HELPED THE DISADVANTAGED PEOPLE DIANA HAD ALWAYS CHAMPIONED.
42
HH

DIANA PRINCESS OF WALES
HER LOVING WORK WITH AIDS PATIENTS CHANGED THE WORLD!
ACCORDING TO ONE SENIOR FUNDRAISER, HER EFFECT ON CHARITY IS MORE SIGNIFICANT THAN ANY OTHER PERSON IN THE 20TH CENTURY.
WHEN YOU SEE SOMEONE IN PAIN, DON'T LOOK AWAY.
THEY NEED YOUR HELP.

It's your turn now.
The world needs more kindness,
and it certainly needs more empathy.
Compassion is a sign of strength.

Every person you meet is going through something that you can't see.

You won't be able to solve every problem, but when you open your arms and listen with love, you can make sure no one feels alone.

I am Princess Diana.
I lead from the heart.

“Anywhere I see suffering, that is where I want to be, doing what I can.”
—Princess Diana

Timeline

JULY 1, 1961	NOVEMBER 1977	JULY 29, 1981	JUNE 21, 1982	SEPTEMBER 15, 1984
Born the Honourable Diana Frances Spencer in Norfolk, England	Meets Prince Charles for the first time	Marries Prince Charles	Prince William is born	Prince Harry is born

Age 10

Kensington Gardens, 1994

With Angola land mine victims, 1997

NOVEMBER 1989	DECEMBER 1992	AUGUST 28, 1996	JANUARY 15, 1997	AUGUST 31, 1997
Visits leprosy hospital in Indonesia	Separates from Prince Charles	Finalizes divorce with Prince Charles	Visits mine field in Angola	Dies in a car crash in Paris, France

For my mother and daughter,
Teri and Lila,
strong women who are
unapologetically themselves
–B.M.

For Audra,
the most empathetic and
compassionate person I know
–C.E.

For historical accuracy, we used Princess Diana's actual words whenever possible. For more of her true voice, we recommend and acknowledge the below works. Special thanks to Andrew Morton for his input on early drafts.

SOURCES

Diana: Her True Story—In Her Own Words by Andrew Morton (Simon & Schuster, 2017)
"Diana Revealed" interviews with Peter Settelen (2006), available on YouTube

FURTHER READING FOR KIDS

Who Was Princess Diana? by Ellen Labrecque (Penguin Workshop, 2017)

ROCKY POND BOOKS
An imprint of Penguin Random House LLC
1745 Broadway, New York, NY 10019
penguinrandomhouse.com

First published in the United States of America by Rocky Pond Books, 2026

Photo on page 38 by Terence Donovan, Camera Press London; photo of Diana as a girl by Spen/AL, Camera Press London; photo of Diana in Angola by Tim Graham/Getty Images; photo of Diana in a black dress by Jayne Fincher/Getty Images

Colored by Jason Henry with Christopher Eliopoulos
Design by Omou Barry • Text set in Triplex
The illustrator created the artwork for this book using Wacom Cintiq and Clip Studio Paint with custom pencils and brushes.

Library of Congress Cataloging-in-Publication Data is available.

Manufactured in China
TOPL

ISBN 9780593533512
1 3 5 7 9 10 8 6 4 2

The authorized representative in the EU for product safety and compliance is Penguin Random House Ireland, Morrison Chambers, 32 Nassau Street, Dublin D02 YH68, Ireland, https://eu-contact.penguin.ie.

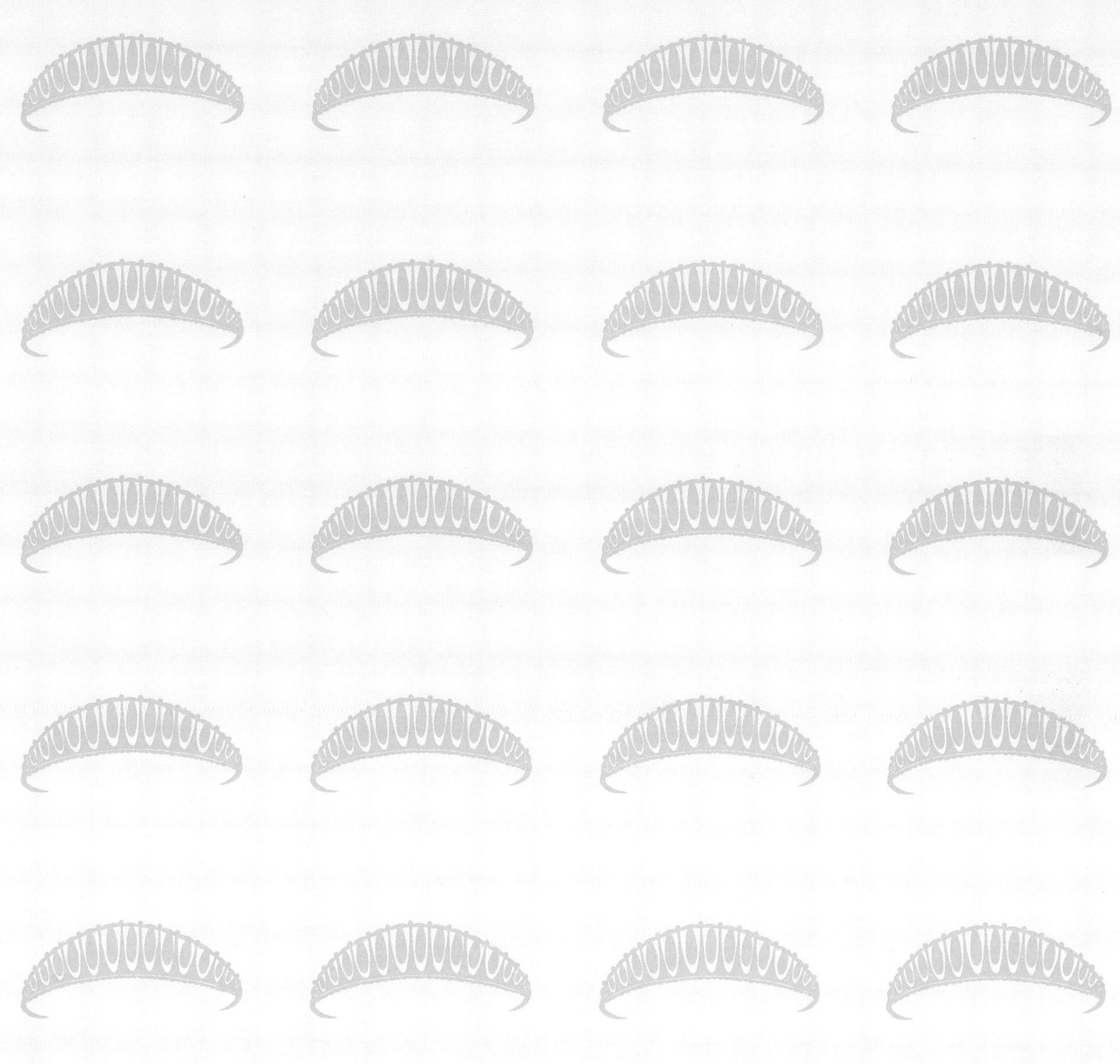